ANY TIME YOU FIRE UP YOUR COMPUTER, I BET YOU SEE GOOGLE. IT'S EITHER THE FIRST PAGE YOU GO TO, OR THERE'S A SEARCH FUNCTION ON YOUR TOOLBAR. EITHER WAY, YOU KNOW *GOOGLE* AND YOU USE IT FREQUENTLY. YOU MIGHT HAVE EVEN USED IT RIGHT BEFORE READING THIS. BUT DO YOU KNOW THE MEN BEHIND THE PHENOMENA? DO YOU KNOW *SERGEY BRIN* AND *LARRY PAGE?*

HE ATTENDED A MONTESSORI GRADE SCHOOL IN MARYLAND BUT CONTINUED HIS EDUCATION AT HOME WITH HIS FATHER, LEARNING MATH AND HIS RUSSIAN LANGUAGE SKILLS. THAT HELPED HIM ALONG HIS PATH AS HE...

ENROLLED AND STUDIED AT THE UNIVERSITY OF MARYLAND. HE STUDIED COMPUTER SCIENCE AND MATH AND WHEN HE GRADUATED IN 1993 WITH HONORS, JUST A FEW MONTHS SHORT OF HIS 20TH BIRTHDAY.

SERGEY ENROLLED FOR HIS GRADUATE DEGREE AT STANFORD IN COMPUTER SCIENCE. HE RECEIVED A FELLOWSHIP FROM THE NATIONAL SCIENCE FOUNDATION. BUT GOING TO STANFORD WASN'T THE ONLY IMPORTANT THING THAT HAPPENED...

AS HE MET LARRY PAGE, HIS GOOGLE COLLABORATOR, AT AN ORIENTATION AT STANFORD.

WE'RE BOTH KIND OF OBNOXIOUS.

BEFORE WE GET TO THE CREATION OF GOOGLE, THERE'S MORE TO BE SAID ABOUT SERGEY BEYOND JUST HIS FOUNDING OF GOOGLE. IN 2007, HE MARRIED ANNE WOJCICKI, A BIOTECH ANALYST AND YALE GRAD. THEY WERE MARRIED IN THE BAHAMAS...

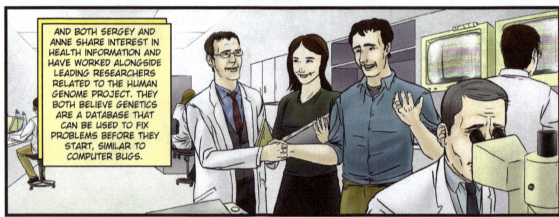

AND BOTH SERGEY AND ANNE SHARE INTEREST IN HEALTH INFORMATION AND HAVE WORKED ALONGSIDE LEADING RESEARCHERS RELATED TO THE HUMAN GENOME PROJECT. THEY BOTH BELIEVE GENETICS ARE A DATABASE THAT CAN BE USED TO FIX PROBLEMS BEFORE THEY START, SIMILAR TO COMPUTER BUGS.

IN 2008, SERGEY'S MOTHER EUGENIA WAS DIAGNOSED WITH PARKINSON'S DISEASE AND INSTEAD OF HIDING BEHIND FEAR, HE MADE A LARGE DONATION TO THE UNIVERSITY OF MARYLAND SCHOOL OF MEDICINE WHERE HIS MOM WAS BEING TREATED AND ALSO LEARNED ABOUT HIS OWN GENETICS. HE LEARNED THAT HE AND HIS MOTHER BOTH POSSESS A MUTATION THAT MAKES THE LIKELIHOOD OF BEING DIAGNOSED WITH PARKINSON'S MUCH HIGHER.

HE DIDN'T HIDE OR COWER. HE FACED FORWARD AND ATTACKED THE POTENTIAL FOR THIS DISEASE WITH THE KNOWLEDGE THAT HE NOW HAD. ATTACKING A PROBLEM HEADFIRST IS SOMETHING SERGEY ALWAYS DOES, AND HE UNDERSTANDS THAT KNOWLEDGE IS THE MOST IMPORTANT STEP TOWARD PREVENTION.

HE HAS APPEARED ON A NUMBER OF TELEVISION PROGRAMS TO DISCUSS HIS BELIEFS AND HIS WORK WITH GOOGLE AND ELSEWHERE. HE'S BEEN ON CHARLIE ROSE, CNN, CNBC, AND MANY OTHERS.

HE'S AN INVESTOR IN TESLA MOTORS...

HE INVESTED $4.5 MILLION IN SPACE ADVENTURES, A SPACE TOURISM COMPANY THAT HAS SENT 7 PEOPLE INTO SPACE. HIS INVESTMENT ALSO ACTS AS HIS OWN CHANCE TO GET TO GO INTO SPACE IN THE NEAR FUTURE.

HE'S ALSO A MEMBER OF AmBAR, A GROUP WHOSE MEMBERS ARE ALL RUSSIAN-SPEAKING PROFESSIONALS. HE'S GIVEN MANY SPEECHES TO THESE GATHERED MEMBERS AT DIFFERENT EVENTS OVER TIME.

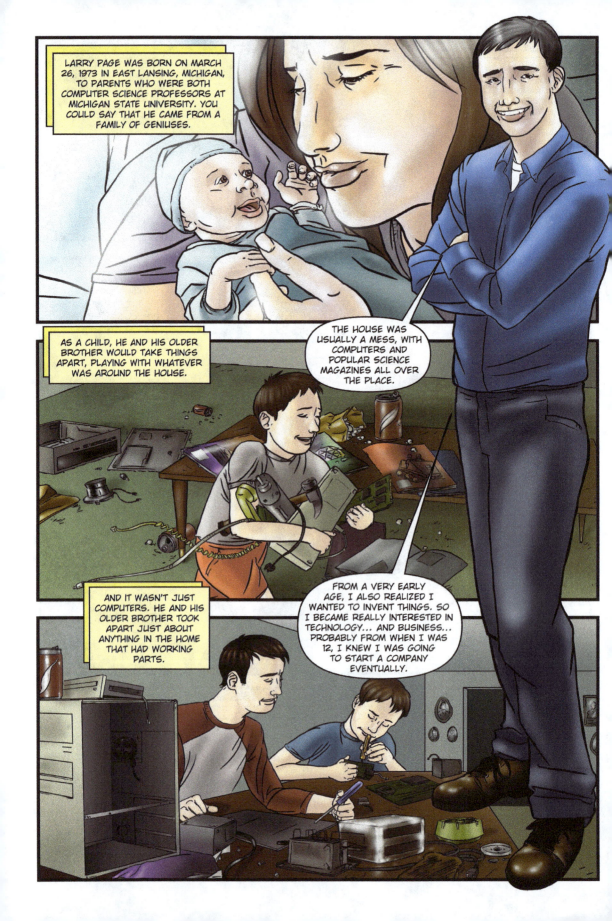

LARRY PAGE WAS BORN ON MARCH 26, 1973 IN EAST LANSING, MICHIGAN, TO PARENTS WHO WERE BOTH COMPUTER SCIENCE PROFESSORS AT MICHIGAN STATE UNIVERSITY. YOU COULD SAY THAT HE CAME FROM A FAMILY OF GENIUSES.

THE HOUSE WAS USUALLY A MESS, WITH COMPUTERS AND POPULAR SCIENCE MAGAZINES ALL OVER THE PLACE.

AS A CHILD, HE AND HIS OLDER BROTHER WOULD TAKE THINGS APART, PLAYING WITH WHATEVER WAS AROUND THE HOUSE.

AND IT WASN'T JUST COMPUTERS. HE AND HIS OLDER BROTHER TOOK APART JUST ABOUT ANYTHING IN THE HOME THAT HAD WORKING PARTS.

FROM A VERY EARLY AGE, I ALSO REALIZED I WANTED TO INVENT THINGS. SO I BECAME REALLY INTERESTED IN TECHNOLOGY... AND BUSINESS... PROBABLY FROM WHEN I WAS 12, I KNEW I WAS GOING TO START A COMPANY EVENTUALLY.

AFTER ATTENDING THE OKEMOS MONTESSORI SCHOOL IN MICHIGAN AND EAST LANSING HIGH SCHOOL, HE MOVED ONTO THE UNIVERSITY OF MICHIGAN.

HE RECEIVED A BACHELOR OF SCIENCE IN COMPUTER ENGINEERING AT THE UNIVERSITY OF MICHIGAN WITH HONORS.

HE WAS THE PRESIDENT OF THE ETA KAPPA NU FRATERNITY...

AS WELL AS A MEMBER OF THE MAIZE & BLUE SOLAR TEAM WHILE HE CONTINUED HIS STUDIES AT MICHIGAN.

ONCE HE FINISHED HIS DEGREE WITH HONORS AT THE UNIVERSITY OF MICHIGAN, HE ATTENDED STANFORD UNIVERSITY TO GET HIS MASTER'S DEGREE IN COMPUTER SCIENCE.

WHEN HE ENROLLED FOR HIS PH.D. PROGRAM AT STANFORD, HE MET SERGEY BRIN AT AN ORIENTATION FOR NEW STUDENTS. THE TWO WOULD SOON WORK WELL TOGETHER, BUT OUR STORY ON LARRY DOESN'T JUST STOP HERE.

HE QUICKLY BEGAN WORK ON HIS DISSERTATION BUT HAD TROUBLE, INITIALLY, WITH FINDING THE RIGHT PATH. HIS FIRST IDEA, WHICH WAS DISCUSSED AND ENCOURAGED BY HIS SUPERVISOR, WAS THE PROPERTIES OF THE WORLD WIDE WEB IN RELATION TO MATHEMATICS.

HE BEGAN TO UNDERSTAND HOW WEB PAGES WERE CONNECTED, LOOKING AT HOW CERTAIN PAGES LINKED TOGETHER.

HE NICKNAMED THE PROJECT BACKRUB, WHICH WOULD EXPLAIN THAT THE INTERNET WAS ESSENTIALLY BASED ON CITATION. IT WAS A HUGE UNDERTAKING, AND IT BROUGHT THE ATTENTION OF SERGEY BRIN.

"THIS WAS THE MOST EXCITING PROJECT, BOTH BECAUSE IT TACKLED THE WEB, WHICH REPRESENTS HUMAN KNOWLEDGE, AND BECAUSE I LIKED LARRY."

IT WOULD BE THE BASIS FOR HOW GOOGLE BEGAN, BUT THIS ISN'T WHERE LARRY'S STORY ENDS.

IN 2007, HE MARRIED LUCINDA SOUTHWORTH, A RESEARCH SCIENTIST. THE TWO WERE MARRIED IN THE CARIBBEAN AND HAVE SINCE HAD A CHILD TOGETHER.

JUST LIKE SERGEY, HE IS ALSO AN INVESTOR IN THE TESLA MOTOR COMPANY, THE CREATORS OF THE TESLA ROADSTER.

LARRY AND SERGEY HAVE ALSO ACTED AS FILM PRODUCERS, ON SUCH FILMS AS BROKEN ARROWS. IT IS JUST ONE OF MANY OF THEIR EXCITING BUSINESS VENTURES TOGETHER OR APART.

BUT OF COURSE, THEIR MOST IMPORTANT VENTURE TOGETHER HAS BEEN THE CREATION OF GOOGLE. IT STARTED FROM THEIR WORK TOGETHER ON BACKRUB, IN WHICH THEY WORKED ON A PAGE RANK ALGORITHM WHICH WOULD MEASURE THE IMPORTANCE OF ANY GIVEN WEB PAGE.

ORIGINALLY RUNNING UNDER THE STANFORD UNIVERSITY WEBSITE AS GOOGLE.STANFORD.EDU, GOOGLE WAS NAMED THIS AS IT IS A MISSPELLING OF THE WORD GOOGOL WHICH IS THE NUMBER 1 FOLLOWED BY 100 ZEROES. IT WAS THEIR WAY OF SAYING THAT THEIR WEB SERVICE WOULD PROVIDE A HUGE QUANTITY OF INFORMATION TO THE USER.

AND IT WAS ORIGINALLY VERY SIMPLE IN ITS WEBPAGE DESIGN. GOOGLE WASN'T ADVANCED BECAUSE THE TWO CREATORS, SERGEY AND LARRY, WEREN'T THAT ADVANCED AT WRITING HTML.

IN 1997, GOOGLE'S DOMAIN NAME WAS REGISTERED AND THEY WERE INCORPORATED BY SEPTEMBER OF 1998. THEY WERE ORIGINALLY HOUSED IN SUSAN WOJCICKI'S GARAGE, BUT THAT WOULDN'T LAST TOO TERRIBLY LONG FOR THEM.

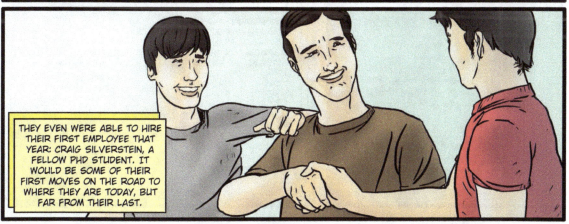

THEY EVEN WERE ABLE TO HIRE THEIR FIRST EMPLOYEE THAT YEAR: CRAIG SILVERSTEIN, A FELLOW PHD STUDENT. IT WOULD BE SOME OF THEIR FIRST MOVES ON THE ROAD TO WHERE THEY ARE TODAY, BUT FAR FROM THEIR LAST.

PRETTY EARLY ON, THEY RECEIVED $100,000 OF FUNDING FROM THE CO-FOUNDER OF SUN MICROSYSTEMS EVEN BEFORE THEY WERE INCORPORATED. BUT SERGEY AND LARRY ALSO DECIDED, WHILE THEY WERE STILL STUDENTS IN 1999, THAT GOOGLE WAS TAKING UP TOO MUCH OF THEIR TIME. THEY HAD NO TIME TO STUDY AND NO TIME FOR PRETTY MUCH ANYTHING ELSE, SO THEY BEGAN TO TAKE MEETINGS WITH BUSINESSMEN SUCH AS EXCITE CEO GEORGE BELL, OFFERING TO SELL HIM THE COMPANY FOR $1 MILLION. THANKFULLY FOR SERGEY AND LARRY, THE CEO DECLINED THE OFFER.

THEY DID END UP OBTAINING FUNDING, WITH UP TO $25 MILLION COMING MAINLY FROM VENTURE CAPITAL FIRMS LIKE SEQUOIA CAPITAL AND KLEINER PERKINS CAULFIELD AND BYERS.

ONCE FUNDING STARTED TO RISE, THEY WERE ABLE TO MOVE FROM THEIR HUMBLE GARAGE BEGINNINGS TO A MORE SUITABLE PLACE OF BUSINESS, MOVING INTO AN OFFICE IN PALO ALTO, CALIFORNIA. THEY WOULDN'T LAST LONG IN THESE OFFICES, AS GOOGLE CONTINUED TO GROW.

AS GOOGLE GREW, DESPITE THEIR BEST INTEN-TIONS, SO DID THE NEED FOR ADVERTISEMENTS. THE ADS WERE SOLD BASED ON KEYWORDS IN A SEARCH AND WOULD BE TEXT-BASED ONLY.

Sponsored Links

Sasquatch Feeder
Find Bird Feeders, squirrel za
and more at www.feedersfor
http://www.feedersforfuzzyfriends.com

Squirrel Zapper
Find Bird Feeders, squirrel za
and more at www.feedersforf
http://www.feedersforfuzzyfriends.com

Edible Sandals

AMONG OTHER MAJOR EVENTS IN THE FIRST COUPLE YEARS OF THE DEVELOPMENT AND GROWTH OF GOOGLE, THEY WERE GRANTED A PATENT ON THE PAGERANK MECHANISM, LISTING LARRY PAGE AS THE INVENTOR AND ASSIGNED TO STANFORD UNIVERSITY. IT WAS ANOTHER IN A LONG LIST OF THINGS THAT HELPED TO LEGITIMIZE THE SMALL BUT BLOSSOMING COMPANY.

AS THE COMPANY CONTINUED TO GROW AND EXPANDED PAST THE BOUNDARIES OF TWO MORE SITES, THEY FOUND THEIR LONGEST LASTING HOME, IN MOUNTAIN VIEW, CALIFORNIA.

Google

CALLED THE GOOGLEPLEX, THIS HOME HOUSES THE HEADQUARTERS OF GOOGLE IN CALIFORNIA. IT IS A HUGE COMPLEX OF BUILDINGS THAT FEATURES PIANOS, EXERCISE BALLS, BICYCLES, LAVA LAMPS, AND SO MUCH MORE. BASICALLY, IT SOUNDS AND LOOKS LIKE THE PLACE YOU AND EVERYONE ELSE WOULD LOVE TO WORK.

ALL EMPLOYEES ARE ALLOWED USAGE OF THE EXERCISE ROOMS. BUT THESE AREN'T ONLY FOR WORKING OUT. YOU CAN WASH AND DRY YOUR CLOTHES THERE, YOU CAN GET A MASSAGE, AND...

THEY CAN ALSO PLAY VIDEO GAMES OR POOL. HOW ANYONE THERE GETS ANY WORK DONE IS BEYOND ME, BUT IT MUST BE BECAUSE THEY HAVE SO MUCH FUN THAT THEY NEVER WANT TO LEAVE.

GOOGLE HAS BEEN NAMED THE MOST DESIRABLE AND MOST ATTRACTIVE EMPLOYER TO GRADUATING STUDENTS ACROSS THE COUNTRY. OBVIOUSLY, MOST PEOPLE CAN SEE THAT THEIR INFORMALITIES AND THEIR WORK ETHIC ARE THE REASONS FOR THIS.

SOME OF THE PRINCIPLES OF GOOGLE INCLUDE: YOU CAN BE SERIOUS WITHOUT A SUIT...

WORK SHOULD BE CHALLENGING AND THE CHALLENGE SHOULD BE FUN...

AND YOU CAN MAKE MONEY WITHOUT BEING EVIL.

AND GOOGLE'S INVENTORS AND CHAIRMAN, SERGEY, LARRY AND ERIC, RESPECTIVELY, DO THEIR BEST TO FOLLOW ALL OF THESE PRINCIPLES. AFTER GOOGLE'S INITIAL PUBLIC OFFERING, THE PERFORMANCE OF THEIR STOCK WENT THROUGH THE ROOF, ALLOWING THEM TO BE COMPENSATED QUITE HIGHLY BY THEIR STOCKS. BECAUSE OF THIS, THEY ALL REQUESTED THAT THEIR SALARIES BE CUT TO $1, AND EVERY TIME THE QUESTION OF A RAISE OR AN INCREASE IN SALARY HAS BEEN BROUGHT UP, ALL THREE HAVE TURNED IT DOWN.

IN THEIR QUEST TO NEVER DO EVIL, GOOGLE SUPPORTS NET NEUTRALITY. THEY EVEN HAVE A GUIDE TO IT, WHICH SAYS:

NET NEUTRALITY IS ABOUT EQUAL ACCESS TO THE INTERNET. IN OUR VIEW, THE BROADBAND CARRIERS SHOULD NOT BE PERMITTED TO USE THEIR MARKET POWER TO DISCRIMINATE AGAINST COMPETING APPLICATIONS OR CONTENT. JUST AS TELEPHONE COMPANIES ARE NOT PERMITTED TO TELL CONSUMERS WHO THEY CAN CALL OR WHAT THEY CAN SAY, BROADBAND CARRIERS SHOULD NOT BE ALLOWED TO USE THEIR MARKET POWER TO CONTROL ACTIVITY ONLINE.

Mr. Cerf

AND IN 2006, VINCENT CERF, A CO-INVENTOR OF INTERNET PROTOCOL AND THE CHIEF INTERNET EVANGELIST AND VICE PRESIDENT OF GOOGLE, TESTIFIED BEFORE CONGRESS ABOUT NET NEUTRALITY.

ALLOWING BROADBAND CARRIERS TO CONTROL WHAT PEOPLE SEE AND DO ONLINE WOULD FUNDAMENTALLY UNDERMINE THE PRINCIPLES THAT HAVE MADE THE INTERNET SUCH A SUCCESS.

CONTINUING THEIR PLANS TO SAVE THE WORLD BY ANY MEANS THAT THEY CAN, GOOGLE FORMED GOOGLE.ORG, A NOT-FOR-PROFIT ORGANIZATION THAT THEY GAVE $1 BILLION AS A START-UP FUND.

ONE OF THEIR FIRST PROJECTS WAS AN ELECTRIC HYBRID CAR THAT WOULD GET 100 MILES PER GALLON AND THEIR FIRST EXECUTIVE DIRECTOR WAS DR. LARRY BRILLIANT. THEIR MISSION, WHICH IS STILL ONGOING UNDER CURRENT DIRECTOR MEGAN SMITH, IS TO CREATE AWARENESS ON GLOBAL PUBLIC HEALTH, CLIMATE CHANGE, AND GLOBAL POVERTY.

GOOGLE HAS EVEN EMPLOYED IDEAS THAT SOME MIGHT FIND A BIT CONFUS-ING OR ODD IN ORDER TO LOWER THEIR CARBON FOOTPRINT. THEY ANNOUNCED PLANS IN 2006 TO INSTALL SOLAR PANELS ON THEIR BUILDINGS IN ORDER TO PROVIDE 30% OF THEIR ENERGY NEEDS ON CAMPUS. WHILE THAT WAS NEITHER CONFUSING NOR ODD, THEY DID ALSO EMPLOY THE USE OF HERDS OF GOATS TO KEEP THE GRASS AROUND THE CAMPUS SHORT. THIS WAS USED TO CUT BACK ON THE USE OF MOWERS AND THEIR GAS USAGE AS WELL AS TO KEEP THE GRASS SHORT TO CUT BACK ON THE POSSIBILITY OF BUSH FIRES.

IN SPITE OF THEIR WORK TO HELP SAVE THE ENVIRONMENT OR CUT BACK ON THEIR OWN CARBON FOOTPRINT, GOOGLE WAS ACCUSED OF BEING AN ENERGY GLUTTON AND OF USING THESE VERY PUBLIC CAMPAIGNS AS A WAY TO COVER UP THEIR MASSIVE ENERGY USAGE.

Google: Energy Gluttons
by Johnny Expectorant
Space Tea
by Irena M

TO GO ALONG WITH THE CORPORATE CULTURE OF HAVING FUN AND ENJOYING WHAT YOU DO, OVER THE YEARS, GOOGLE HAS EMPLOYED BOTH EASTER EGGS AND APRIL FOOL'S JOKES AS PART OF ITS ONGOING CORPORATE IDENTITY. YOU CAN MAKE THE GOOGLE HOMEPAGE DO A BARREL ROLL, WE'VE SEEN THE HOMEPAGE'S NAME CHANGED TO TOPEKA IN ORDER OF THE NEW GOOGLE FIBER PROJECT, YOU CAN USE YOUR BODY TO SEND EMAILS (BUT ONLY ON APRIL 1ST THROUGH GMAIL MOTION), AND YOU CAN EVEN GET THE ANSWER TO THE ULTIMATE QUESTION OF LIFE, THE UNIVERSE AND EVERYTHING. AND THAT ANSWER IS 42.

ERIC SCHMIDT, CEO OF GOOGLE, HAS BEEN A VOCAL SUPPORTER OF BOTH GOOGLE AND NOT ONLY ITS FUTURE, BUT ALSO THE FUTURE OF THE INTERNET.

THE GOAL IS TO ENABLE GOOGLE USERS TO BE ABLE TO ASK THE QUESTION SUCH AS 'WHAT SHALL I DO TOMORROW?' AND 'WHAT JOB SHALL I TAKE?'

GOOGLE HAS FACED CRITICISMS FOR SOME OF ITS VIEWS ON PRIVACY AS WELL. IT HAS BEEN RANKED AS HOSTILE TO PRIVACY BY PRIVACY INTERNATIONAL.

IF YOU HAVE SOMETHING THAT YOU DON'T WANT ANYONE TO KNOW, MAYBE YOU SHOULDN'T BE DOING IT IN THE FIRST PLACE. IF YOU REALLY NEED THAT KIND OF PRIVACY, THE REALITY IS THAT SEARCH ENGINES – INCLUDING GOOGLE – DO RETAIN THIS INFORMATION FOR SOME TIME AND IT'S IMPORTANT, FOR EXAMPLE, THAT WE ARE ALL SUBJECT IN THE UNITED STATES TO THE PATRIOT ACT AND IT IS POSSIBLE THAT ALL INFORMATION COULD BE MADE AVAILABLE TO THE AUTHORITIES.

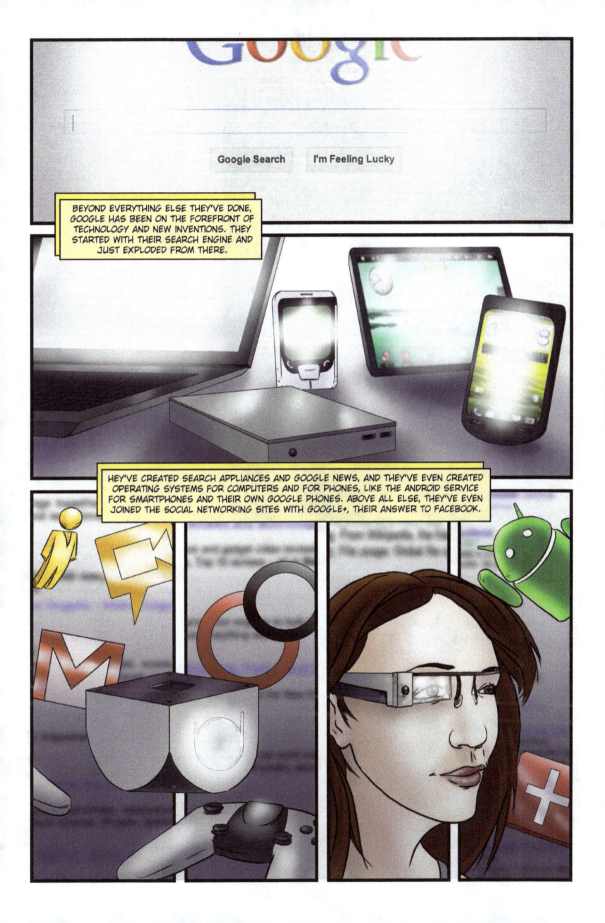

BUT THE FOUNDERS OF GOOGLE, LARRY PAGE AND SERGEY BRIN, HAVE DONE MORE THAN JUST WORK ON GOOGLE. THEIR WORK HAS GIVEN THEM NUMEROUS AWARDS AND RECOGNITIONS, INCLUDING THE MIT TECHNOLOGY REVIEW, HONORARY MBAS, MARCONI FOUNDATION PRIZES, AND BEING LISTED IN FORBES MAGAZINE AS BOTH POWERFUL PEOPLE AND SOME OF THE RICHEST PEOPLE IN THE WORLD.

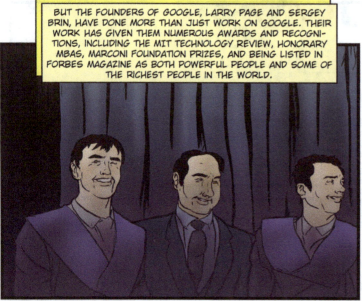

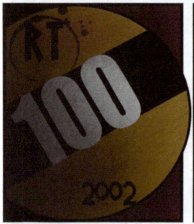

13 Sergey Brin

13 Larry Page

AND NO MATTER WHAT THE TWO MEN DO, THE WORLD WILL STOP AND TAKE NOTICE. AS THE INVENTORS OF GOOGLE, THEY HAVE GIVEN THE WORLD SOMETHING THAT MAKES ALL INTERNET SEARCHES EASIER AND MORE ENJOYABLE, WHERE KNOWLEDGE IS JUST A CLICK AWAY. AND AS THINGS CHANGE AND THE WORLD CHANGES AROUND THEM, LARRY PAGE AND SERGEY BRIN HAVE PROVEN THAT THEY ARE NOT GOING TO SIT IDLY BY AND LET THE WORLD CHANGE AROUND THEM. THEY ARE GOING TO CONTINUE TO INNOVATE AND CHANGE WITH THE WORLD, AND GOOGLE WILL ALWAYS BE ON THE FOREFRONT OF THAT CHANGE.

THE END

CW Cooke ———————————— Writer

Greg Freeland II ———————————— Penciler

Greg Freeland II ———————————— Colorist

Warren Montgomery ———————————— Letterer

Darren G. Davis ———————————— Editor

Darren G. Davis
Publisher

Jason Schultz
Vice President

Jackie Stickley
New Business Development

Jarred Weisfeld
Literary Manager

Kailey Marsh
Entertainment Manager

Maggie Jessup
Publicity

Nikki Borror
Coordinator

Warren Montgomery
Production

www.bluewaterprod.com

#ERASEHATE WITH THE MATTHEW SHEPARD FOUNDATION

With your donated dollars and volunteer hours, we work tirelessly to erase hate from every corner of America through our programs.

SPEAKING ENGAGEMENTS

Since Matt's death in 1998, Judy and Dennis have been determined to prevent others from similar tragedies. By sharing their story, they are able to carry on Matt's legacy.

HATE CRIMES REPORTING

Our work to improve reporting includes conducting trainings for law enforcement agencies, building relationships between community leaders and law enforcement, and developing policy reform in reporting practices.

LARAMIE PROJECT

MSF offers support to productions of The Laramie Project, which depicts the events leading up to and after Matt's murder. It remains one of the most performed plays in America.

MATTHEW'S PLACE

MatthewsPlace.com is a blog designed to provide young LGBTQ+ people with an outlet for their voices. From finance to health to love and dating, and everything in between, our writers contribute excellent material.

Erase Hate

Matthew Shepard Foundation
embracing diversity